BEYOND BEANS ON TOAST

BEYOND BEANS ON TOAST

CLAIRE POVEY

Text copyright © 2015 by Claire Povey
Recipes copyright © 2015 by Alex Reynolds
Photographs copyright © 2015 by Ben Stoney Photography, with food prepared by Alex Reynolds

First published in Great Britain in 2015

British Library Cataloguing in Publication Data
A record for this book is available from the British Library

ISBN: 978-1-910587-07-2

Designed by Diane Warnes

Printed in China

10Publishing, a division of 10ofthose.com
9D Centurion Court, Farington, Leyland, PR25 3UQ, England
Email: info@10ofthose.com
Website: www.10ofthose.com

WHAT'S INSIDE

INTRODUCTION

Moving out, settling in, collecting a reading lis the size of your arm and learning to wield you wok like it's a weapon — these are all norma ingredients to starting life at uni.

The months ahead will be full of change, some you may have expected (like navigating you way around the town you'll be calling 'home' and some that may come as a surprise (like sitting next to an exchange student from South Carolina, who is adjusting to the climate b wearing all the contents of his suitcase).

If you're excited and daunted by the challenge ahead, then this little book is for you. It's packed with tasty recipes donated by a professiona chef to keep you well fed on a budget. It's crammed with tips as you prepare for the changes to come and different people to meet And it's full of stories from students who discovered a new life at university that went fa *beyond* beans on toast!

TEN THINGS YOU NEVER THOUGHT YOU'D PACK ...

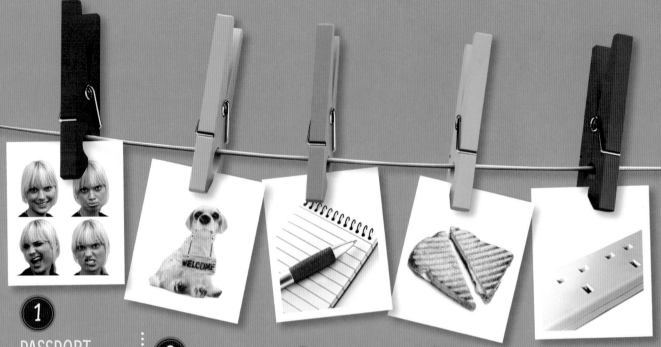

1

PASSPORT PHOTOS

I know it's odd — you may be studying at Kingston, London not Kingston, Jamaica — but you'll be surprised how many passport photos you'll need for ID cards, passes and forms.

2

DOOR STOP

One of these — or a hefty textbook — to keep your door open for the first couple of weeks will help you build friendships.

3

NUMBERS

You need numbers ... for everything! Jot down your national insurance number, your NHS number, your student loan number ... if in doubt, bring it.

4

TOASTIE MAKER

Offering a toastie ... is offering friendship! It is a miracle machine: put in the cheapest bread and the grimmest cheese and, voilà, you get gooey, crispy gorgeousness.

5

EXTENSION LEAD

Get the chunkiest one you can find: how else will you shave, print, heat your straighteners and play the Xbox all at once?

... beyond your duvet, teddy and laptop

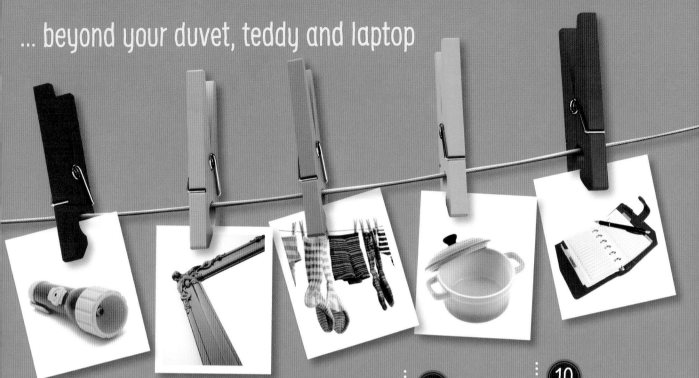

6

TORCH

When the power has gone down and everyone is in 'freak-out' mode, a halo of light will beam from the hall-hero who brought their torch ...

7

FULL-LENGTH MIRROR

Uni rooms usually come with a very small mirror, so if you want to see your bottom half in the first year, take a big one. It will also give a sense of 'space' to your iddy-biddy room.

8

CLOTHES HORSE

Check with your halls first, but unless you want to hang your pants out the window, you'll want somewhere to dry them.

9

CASSEROLE DISH

This isn't for everyone, but if you want to learn the art of cooking en masse and freezing a week's worth of spag bol, curry or the like, it's worth asking for; cooking this way will save you a fortune!

10

FAMILY CALENDAR

Get your mum to write all the 'important' dates in your diary. That way you won't forget Great Aunt Nora's ninetieth birthday card — and it's an easy way to stay in touch!

11

ONE-PAN FRY-UP

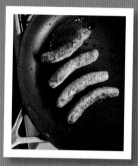

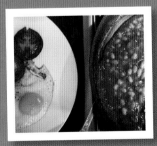

SERVES: 1
PREPARATION: 5 minutes
COOKING: 15–20 minutes
APPROX. COST: £1.05

INGREDIENTS:

1 tbsp oil

1 sausage, cut in half lengthways and the skin removed

2 rashers of bacon

1 tomato, halved

1 egg

½ tin of baked beans

1. Place the oil in the pan and heat to a medium heat. Add your sausage halves and brown them.

2. Next add your bacon and tomato halves. Cook for 4–5 minutes, turning occasionally, allowing the bacon to crisp up and the tomatoes to caramelise.

3. Add your egg to the pan and fry for 3–4 minutes until the egg white is fully cooked.

4. Transfer all these items to your plate before adding the beans to your pan. Stir until hot, then add to the rest of your meal.

Serve with toast.

CHEF'S TIP:

The sausages are halved to speed up the process. If you want them whole, you need to make sure they are fully cooked right to the middle. The best way to check this is to cut them open and with your knuckle make sure the middle is piping hot.

VARIATIONS:

If you like, you could add some mushrooms to this, slicing them and adding with the tomato.

CHARLOTTE'S STORY

CHARLOTTE ELLIS
Lancaster University
**English Literature
and History**

I AM CURRENTLY IN MY LAST YEAR AT UNI. I REMEMBER BEING IN THE SIXTH FORM AND FEELING BOTH INCREDIBLY EXCITED AND VERY DAUNTED ABOUT LEAVING. *WOULD I MAKE FRIENDS? COULD I HACK THE COURSE? WHAT ABOUT EVERYONE I'D BE LEAVING BEHIND? ...*

There has been so much change – and it's been a bit of a journey for me in many ways. Firstly, the independence is incredible. I can go out when I want and eat what I want! I have also made loads of fantastic friends and my course is packed with variety and lots of coursework (which means less exams – woo!). I have actually found it less stressful than A levels.

The other huge changes have been having time and space to find answers to my big questions about life. At sixth form, some of my closest friends were Christians. I would have said I was a Christian too (I was christened as a baby!) but there was something very different about what they believed and how they spoke about it. As far as I knew (not that I had been), 'church' was the epitome of boring.

When I got to uni, I started reading a Gideon's New Testament. I thought it was the best time to look into Christianity as no one knew me and people wouldn't have preconceived ideas about me. I'd heard about the Christian Union through flyers, so I emailed them and asked if I could grill someone with my questions. I started meeting a girl for coffee each week and we went through Luke's Gospel with the Uncover course. Over time, I started understanding more — but it wasn't until we got to the parable of 'The Lost Son'[1] that things clicked. Here was God, a loving Father, with his arms open, inviting me to embrace him and know him personally even though he knew how I had lived my life until then and how I had rejected him. This was not the Christianity I had envisioned — there was feasting and joy and a massive party ... I couldn't quite believe how much God loved me. I started to see that by trusting in Jesus' death on the cross I could be forgiven and brought into a loving relationship with God, like the 'lost son' in the parable. I gave my life to God and started going to church. That was over a year ago now.

There's so much about university life to look forward to, whether you are excited or nervous or a mix — like I was. In many ways it's a fresh start full of new people, experiences and things to learn. Why don't you make space for the 'big questions in life' too?

'MY COURSE IS PACKED WITH VARIETY AND COURSEWORK ... I HAVE ACTUALLY FOUND IT LESS STRESSFUL THAN A LEVELS.'

Uncover is an examination of the evidence about the life and purpose of Jesus Christ. Why don't you check it out?
Go to: **www.uncover.org.uk**

[1] Luke 15:11–32.

PANCAKES

SERVES: 3–4 (makes approx. 6–8 pancakes)
PREPARATION: 15 minutes
COOKING: 30 minutes
APPROX. COST: £0.51 or 15p per person

INGREDIENTS:

60g plain flour
pinch of salt
1 egg
140ml milk
50g butter

1. To make the batter, place the flour and salt in a bowl. Next, add the egg and whisk. Then add a third of the milk at a time and whisk well between each addition. Adding the milk slowly prevents lumps forming.

CHEF'S TIP:

Do you have lumps in your batter? Don't worry! Just pass the mixture through a sieve.

2. Heat a frying pan, then melt a little butter, moving it around to grease the pan. Quickly add enough batter to just cover the base of the pan. I find using a ladle or cup helps with this. After 30 seconds check the underside of the pancake is golden brown. When it is, flip it over and brown the other side.

VARIATIONS:

How about using almond milk for a lactose-free choice? Or for a real chocolate hit, replace 30g of the flour with cocoa powder.

3. Do you want to eat your pancakes all together? If so, turn your oven to 60°C and pile the pancakes up on a baking tray. They'll stay warm while you cook more.

4. Toppings are your choice: lemon and sugar, chocolate and strawberries, cheese and ham ...

KING OF THE KITCHEN

SOON THIS TITLE WILL BE YOURS. KNOWING YOU'LL BE THE MASTER OF YOUR OWN PALATE MAY FILL YOU WITH EXCITEMENT OR DISTURB YOU *AND YOUR MUM* BEYOND BELIEF! FOLLOW THESE TIPS THOUGH, AND YOU'LL KEEP BELLY BUGS AT BAY ...

MONSTERS OF CONTAMINATION:
Some everyday items have a dark side

SCRAP THE SPONGE

The kitchen sponge is the No.1 germ breeder in the home! The moist, micro crevices create a haven for breeding bacteria. To clean with a happy conscience, use an antibacterial washing-up liquid, dry your sponge or dishcloth before using it again and replace it weekly. Cheap cloths are the way to go!

NUKE THE TEA TOWEL

The trusty tea towel is another hot spot for germs. Tame it by hanging it to dry after use and regularly washing it in high heat. Also make sure you keep separate 'hand' and 'tea' towels.

CHOOSE WHERE YOU CHOP

The average chopping board has more bum bacteria on it than a toilet seat. (Nice!) To chop with confidence, use separate boards for raw and cooked meat and always wash them well in hot, antibacterial washing-up liquid.

WASH YOUR MITTS

Our hands are the biggest germ-spreaders. Wash your hands in hot, soapy water before and after preparing food, especially when handling raw meat!

SECURE YOUR SURFACE

Kill any lingering bugs by washing worktops before and after preparing food, especially if you've been dealing with raw meat or eggs. It is worth investing in an antibacterial spray!

- Cool leftovers as quickly as possible (within 90 minutes is great), then cover and put in the fridge.

- Use refrigerated leftovers *within two days*. Before eating, make sure you reheat it – just once – until it's steaming hot!

- If you make a big batch of food, you can cool 'extra portions' and freeze them for another time.

- Defrost leftovers from the freezer thoroughly in the fridge or the microwave. Cook the food within 24 hours and, again, make sure it is steaming hot.

- If something has hit its 'use by' date, check if it's freezable, if it is then freeze it before or on (not after) the date.

- Make sure your fridge is below 5°C to stop food-poisoning bugs growing.

DECODING LABELS

USE BY DATE

This is the most important guide to tell whether food is still safe to eat or not. Though that piece of raw chicken may appear perky, bugs like E.coli and salmonella do not cause food to smell 'off'. So don't dodge the use by date – it's not worth it!

BEST BEFORE DATE

Best before dates are about quality, not safety. The food may be safe to eat past the date but may have lost some pizzazz. Judge with your eyes and nose, chopping off weary-looking bits and binning anything that looks suspect!

VEGETABLE SOUP

SERVES: 4
PREPARATION: 15–20 minutes
COOKING: 20 minutes – 1 hour
APPROX. COST: 71p or 18p per person

INGREDIENTS:

1 tbsp butter or oil

3 carrots, peeled and chopped

½ onion, finely diced

1 clove of garlic, crushed or chopped

water or stock (veg or chicken), enough to cover the vegetables

milk or cream (optional), the quantity depending on how thick you want your soup

salt and pepper

THIS RECIPE CAN BE ADAPTED TO MAKE ANY FLAVOUR SOUP YOU WANT. FOLLOW THE INSTRUCTIONS BUT USE THE VEG YOU WANT INSTEAD. IF YOU DON'T HAVE A BLITZER, JUST CUT THE VEG AS SMALL AS POSSIBLE AND USE A POTATO MASHER TO GIVE YOU A FINISH LIKE A CHUNKY SOUP.

1 In a saucepan melt the butter or oil and add the carrots, onion and garlic. Cook until they are softened, stirring regularly. You can do this bit either quickly in 5 minutes or slowly in 20–30 minutes, but the longer you cook the veg down, the more intense the flavour becomes.

2 When they are softened, add enough hot water or stock so the veg is covered. Boil until everything is fully cooked, stirring occasionally. If the veg are not fully cooked, it will not blitz properly.

3 Blitz the soup up until it is nice and smooth, and for an extra touch add some milk or cream to enrich the flavour and thin it down. If you don't want to add milk, water or stock will also do this. Season to taste.

ALSO, SOUP IS BRILLIANT TO FREEZE, DIVIDED INTO PORTIONS. YOU CAN THEN ENJOY A HOMEMADE LUNCH WITH LITTLE HASSLE.

VARIATIONS:

Try adding coriander or curry powder to this recipe. Or use butternut squash, parsnips, spinach, red pepper, aubergine, peas ... The list goes on.

CHEF'S TIP:

Are you not sure how to check the veg is cooked? Take a piece and eat it; if you have to chew it, it's not ready yet. If you are using a stock cube, instructions for how to dilute it should be on the packaging.

ANTHONY'S STORY

ANTHONY DEMETRIOU
University of Nottingham
Politics

WHEN I SET OFF FOR UNIVERSITY, I WAS EXCITED. I MADE FRIENDS QUICKLY AND MY COURSE WAS GREAT. GETTING GOOD DRUG CONNECTIONS WAS EASY AND THERE WERE GIRLS EVERYWHERE. I GOT VERY INTO GOING OUT AND SMASHING IT.

My choices of drug became more exotic and the quantities became more reckless. Outwardly, everything looked fine. I felt I was pretty cool — I had made the right friends and in a way I was having a good time. But inside I was growing empty. I started to do things which surprised even me, like cheating on my girlfriend and allowing my relationship with my parents to deteriorate. I would wake up with a heavy burden of guilt and the fear of someone beginning to lose control. These feelings grew in me like mould left to grow in the dark — yet now and then, I would remember things that my friend (who I had now lost contact with) had told me about Jesus.

One night, I was back home from uni, alone in my room. I had a habit at this point of buying some weed every day, finishing it and feeling unsatisfied. My mind and body were in a very bad shape and I was completely unprepared for the exams I would soon have to sit. I knew I needed help but I couldn't help myself. I thought I had nothing to lose so I would ask Jesus to help me. I told him I was sorry I had ignored him all this time and that I was in trouble. I asked him to help, even though I'd done so many bad things.

Immediately my hairs stood up and it felt as though I was being filled up with water. I flicked open the Bible I had been given and the page fell open on 'Blessed are the poor in spirit, for theirs is the kingdom of heaven ...'[2] I felt that Jesus was in the room with me, speaking these words.

Something that had been dead inside me came alive that night. In the following weeks, I continued to live life the way I had been, but it all felt different. I was changing from the inside out and began to hate the things I used to love. As God showed me his love, his kindness and his forgiveness, my habit with drugs fell off me. He is so much more real than anything I had known before.

> 'GETTING GOOD DRUG CONNECTIONS WAS EASY AND THERE WERE GIRLS EVERYWHERE.'

[2] Matthew 5:3.

ROAST CHICKEN & CHORIZO

THIS IS A GREAT ROAST THAT CAN BE COOKED IN JUST ONE BAKING TRAY.

Preheat the oven to 180°C.

1 In a baking tray place the chicken drumsticks, potatoes, a pinch of salt and four twists of pepper, then add the oil and toss until covered in oil. Roast in the oven for 30 minutes.

2 Meanwhile, mix all the other ingredients except the parsley together.

3 After 30 minutes pour the mixed ingredients into the baking tray, mix well, then roast for another 30 minutes, until the chicken is crispy and the potatoes are cooked.

Remove from oven, add the parsley and serve.

VARIATIONS: Don't want chicken? Put some pork chops in instead. Or try salmon, adding it when the chorizo goes in but placing it on top of everything so that it will roast nicely. For a veggie option, take the chicken and chorizo out and add more vegetables. If chorizo is too pricey for you, try adding a little more paprika and some bacon.

SERVES: 1
PREPARATION: 10 minutes
COOKING: 1 hour
APPROX. COST: £2.13

INGREDIENTS:

2 chicken drumsticks

8 new potatoes or 3 potatoes peeled and chopped into 4

salt and pepper

2 tbsp oil

60g chorizo, any papery skin removed and chopped

1 tsp smoked paprika

2 tomatoes, each cut into 8

½ pepper, diced

5 olives, halved and pitted

2 cloves of garlic, cut into 4

handful of fresh parsley or 1 tsp of dried parsley

THAI GREEN CURRY

SERVES: 1
PREPARATION: 15 minutes
COOKING: 30 minutes
APPROX. COST: £2.51

INGREDIENTS:

1tbsp oil

1 chicken breast, cut into 10 pieces

1 big tbsp Thai green curry paste

½ tin coconut milk, mixed well

1 tbsp light soy sauce

1 tsp brown sugar

1 lime leaf (optional)

4 baby corn, quartered

handful of mangetout, halved

handful of coriander leaves or ½ tsp dried coriander

juice of ½ lime or 1 tbsp lime juice

1 Place the oil, chicken and paste in a pan and heat, stirring, until the chicken turns white on the outside.

2 Add the coconut milk, soy sauce, sugar and lime leaf, if you're using it, to the pan and bring to a simmer — but don't boil — for 15 minutes.

3 Drop your baby corn and mangetout into the curry and simmer for another 5 minutes.

4 Take the curry off the heat, add your coriander and lime juice, and remove the lime leaf. Season with a little more soy sauce if you think it needs it.

Serve with rice and plenty of the sauce.

VARIATIONS:

This recipe is for chicken but you could do a veggie or fish version too. Prawns would be wonderful with this. Other veg you might like to add to this are courgette, aubergine, pepper, peas, green beans and so on. If you use aubergine, though, make sure you add it to the pan before the other vegetables as it needs longer to cook. If you fancy your curry a little hotter, use red curry paste.

CHEF'S TIP:

You need to be 100% sure your chicken is cooked. To check this, take the biggest piece of chicken you can find and cut it open. If the middle is white and the juices from the chicken run clear, the chicken is cooked. By checking the biggest piece, you know the rest should be cooked too.

BRILLIANT BUDGETING
Advice from CAP

BEING SKINT AT UNI SUCKS. IT'S EXCITING TO SEE YOUR BANK BALANCE SOAR AS YOUR STUDENT LOAN ARRIVES, AND THE TEMPTATION TO SPEND IT ALL IN FRESHERS' WEEK CAN BE HUGE! BUT WHAT YOU DO WITH YOUR MONEY IS IMPORTANT BECAUSE YOU'LL WANT TO GET STUCK IN WHILE YOU'RE AT UNI. YOU DON'T WANT TO END UP STRESSING ABOUT MONEY THROUGHOUT THE YEAR AND LEAVING UNIVERSITY WITH A DEBT THAT LASTS A LIFETIME. BEING IN CONTROL OF YOUR MONEY WILL MAKE A HUGE DIFFERENCE TO YOUR LIFE AT UNI AND BEYOND.

'IN MY FIRST YEAR AT UNIVERSITY THE CAP MONEY STUDENTS COURSE HELPED ME NOT ONLY TO AVOID GETTING INTO DEBT, BUT ALSO TO SAVE ENOUGH TO BUY AN ELECTRIC GUITAR'

PETER

Here are some top tips to be in control of your money:

CREATE A BUDGET

It may sound dull, but without a budget you won't know what you can, and can't, afford.

LIVE ON CASH

Using a set amount of cash each week, rather than cards, will stop you blowing your budget all in one go.

GET A SYSTEM TO MANAGE TERMLY PAYMENTS

Such a system makes it easier to juggle the termly income from your student loan alongside monthly and weekly payments.

INCREASE YOUR INCOME

Make sure that you're not missing out on anything you're entitled to in grants or bursaries. Also could you look at additional part-time work during term-time, or summer internships, to bring in some extra cash?

GET A DEAL

Make sure you make the most of the latest deals in shops, online and with an NUS Extra card as well!

Every year, loads of students across the UK go on a CAP Money Students course to find out how they can budget, save and spend as a student. Why not join them by finding your local course here:

www.capuk.org/i-want-help/cap-money-course/students

'I WORKED PART-TIME AND HAD A SUMMER JOB WHILE I WAS AT UNIVERSITY, AND I STILL ENDED UP SPENDING TO THE BOTTOM OF MY OVERDRAFT. I WISH I KNEW WHERE ALL THAT MONEY WENT.'
CLAIRE

CHILLI CON CARNE

THOUGH THIS RECIPE SERVES ONE, CHILLI CON CARNE IS BRILLIANT AS A FREEZER MEAL. WHY NOT MAKE A BIGGER BATCH, PORTION IT OUT AND FREEZE. THEN WHEN YOU DON'T WANT TO COOK, THERE'S A MEAL WAITING FOR YOU.

SERVES: 1
PREPARATION: 20 minutes
COOKING: 30 minutes – 1 hour
APPROX. COST: £1.20

1 In a deep pan, heat the oil and fry the onion until golden brown.

2 Add the garlic and pepper and fry for 3–4 minutes. The pepper should start to go soft.

3 Add the spices and stir constantly for 2 minutes. This cooks the spices out without them burning. If you get lots of spicy vapour, turn the heat down.

4 Add the mince and break it up into little pieces while it cooks. You may need to turn that heat back up now.

5 Add the purée and keep mixing, as this can easily burn if left at the bottom. Treat this like the spices and mix for 2 minutes.

6 Add the chopped tomatoes and stock. If it doesn't cover the mince, add a little more stock or water so it does.

INGREDIENTS:

1 tbsp oil

½ onion, finely chopped

1 clove of garlic, crushed or chopped

½ pepper, diced

1 tsp hot chilli powder

1 tsp smoked paprika (optional)

100g beef mince

1 tbsp tomato purée

½ tin chopped tomatoes

100ml beef stock

½ tin pre-cooked kidney beans, drained

2 cubes of dark chocolate

salt and pepper

VARIATIONS:

If you want this dish to have a real kick, add a whole chilli in too, finely chopped. Alternatively, you can just add more of the dried spices.

7 Put the lid on (if you have one) and simmer for 20 minutes to an hour depending on how long you have. This tenderises the meat and allows the flavours to blend together. Stir occasionally, and if the liquid is reducing, top it up with water to cover the mince.

8 Five minutes before the end of the cooking time, drop in the kidney beans and chocolate. The chocolate enriches the dish and thickens the sauce slightly. Allow the liquid to reduce now.

Season to taste.

CHEF'S TIP:
You can serve this with rice, a jacket potato or wraps. For a real treat, add some nachos and sour cream on the side.

ED'S STORY

ED[3]
University of Exeter
Business Management

'I THOUGHT IT WAS RIDICULOUS THAT PEOPLE FROM ADVANCED COUNTRIES BELIEVED IN GOD.'

[3] Ed's name has been changed for security reasons.

WHERE'S HOME?

I am from Chengdu, a city in south-western China. It has a huge population!

HOW COME YOU'RE STUDYING IN THE UK?

I chose to study abroad for a new experience and a different perspective on the world. I hope it will broaden my career options later.

HOW HAVE YOU FOUND STUDYING HERE?

English is my second language — so that is difficult in a competitive course. The emphasis on students' creativity and honesty is brilliant, though. I also really enjoy my major.

WHAT HAPPENED TO YOU THIS YEAR?

Something I never thought would happen — I became a Christian. In the past, I thought it was ridiculous that people from advanced countries believed in God. Quite frankly, Christianity confused me. It seemed like superstitious nonsense.

SO HOW DID YOUR OPINION CHANGE?

I went with some friends from 'Global Café' (a great place for international students to hang out) to an event called 'Jesus for Sceptics'. The guy who spoke at this event really answered my questions and I knew I wanted to be a Christian.

HOW HAS JESUS AFFECTED YOUR LIFE?

My parents were really shocked and upset. They rejected me at first. Christianity is seen as a little freaky in China. After I told them more about it, they were still concerned for me, but they have seen the positive affects it has had on my life.

DO YOU THINK IT IS WORTH IT?

Yes. I know in my heart that my thoughts and actions are far from perfect. Yet Jesus gave himself for me, he forgave me, he wants me and he loves me. The relationship between me and Jesus is unshakeable and eternal. Nothing beats that.

WHAT'S NEXT FOR YOU?

I hope I can successfully finish my degree. Then I want to do a Masters. I'm not sure where yet!

> THE RELATIONSHIP BETWEEN ME AND JESUS IS UNSHAKEABLE AND ETERNAL.

Friends International is a Christian organisation that wishes to offer friendship to students who come to study in the UK. They run social events, outings and international cafés, and give support and advice to students as they adjust to British culture. Check out:
www.friendsinternational.org.uk

QUICK PASTA

SERVES: 1
PREPARATION: 10 minutes
COOKING: 10 minutes
APPROX. COST: £1.26

INGREDIENTS:
75g pasta
2 rashers of bacon, sliced
1 tbsp oil
½ pepper, diced
½ courgette, sliced
1 tbsp tinned sweet corn
½ tin chopped tomatoes
cheese, grated

HERE IS A PASTA DISH THAT YOU CAN MAKE YOUR OWN. YOU CAN SWAP ITEMS FOR OTHERS AND STILL HAVE A GREAT DISH. I'VE DONE A SIMPLE DISH USING ITEMS YOU MAY HAVE LEFT OVER IF YOU'VE MADE OTHER DISHES FROM THIS BOOK, BUT AS I'VE SAID BEFORE, HAVE A GO AT SWAPPING OR ADDING OTHER ITEMS.

1. Put a pan of water on to boil. Once boiling, add your pasta, stir it well and cook as long as the instructions tell you to on the packet.

2. Meanwhile, place your bacon in a pan with the oil and gently fry for 2–3 minutes. Then add your pepper, courgette and sweetcorn and soften. When only two minutes are to go before the pasta is cooked, add your chopped tomatoes to the vegetables and bring to the boil.

3. Drain your pasta and stir it into your sauce, season and plate it up, adding your cheese on top.

VARIATIONS:
Try using sausage, chorizo, chicken, prawns or salmon. Experiment with adding peas, olives, beans, grated carrot and spinach. Change the sauce by using a BBQ sauce, pesto or cream cheese. The choices are endless while the method stays the same.

THE 'BEFORE I GO' CHECKLIST

THERE SEEMS TO BE TWO CAMPS OF STUDENT THOUGHT:

1 'I have got every detail in hand and every document sorted, laminated and filed in a designated folder ready for the "moving day".'

2 'I will pack my stuff up and would prefer to panic about the rest when I'm there ...'

THE EARLIER YOU CRACK ON WITH GETTING SOMEWHERE TO LAY YOUR WEARY HEAD, THE MORE OPTIONS WILL BE AVAILABLE

HERE'S WHAT WE HOPE IS A HELPFUL LIST TO ASSIST YOU AS YOU GET READY — IN A HAPPY MEDIUM KIND OF WAY:

1. STUDENT LOAN

This is probably the least exciting and most frustrating job, but apply in time so you have money in your account by the time you start your course.

2. STUDENT BANK ACCOUNT

You can apply for a student account even before your A-level results are out! There are some competitive options with very useful free stuff. Go to **moneysavingexpert.com** for some brilliant advice on choosing a student account. Top tip: don't be tempted to go for the 'what bank is on campus?' option — online banking means the best option for you may not be the closest!

3. ACCOMMODATION

The earlier you crack on with getting somewhere to lay your weary head, the more options will be available, before all the cheaper dorms or rooms with that en suite to die for are taken!

4. REDIRECTING POST

When you have your address sorted, get a shimmy on and redirect your post before there is a three-way snail-mail portal going on between the senders, your mum and your halls.

5. HEALTH STUFF

Before you move, see your home GP and check that all your vaccinations are up to date. Meningitis (and other nasties) can spread quickly in close uni quarters. When you get to uni, make registering with the doc and dentist one of the first things on your list to do!

6. HOLD ON, JIMMY!

Hold back from buying up the entire reading list. Wait till you get there — you'll quickly find out what are the 'must-haves' and what can be borrowed from the library or picked up second-hand at a bargain.

7. TECHY STUFF

Find out if your laptop is compatible with the system at uni or whether you'll need to install a wireless card. Are there any design programs you know you'll need early on?

WHEN YOU GET TO UNI, MAKE REGISTERING WITH THE DOC AND DENTIST ONE OF THE FIRST THINGS ON YOUR LIST TO DO!

CHOCOLATE CAKE IN A CUP

SERVES: 2
PREPARATION: 5 minutes
COOKING: 3 minutes (for 2 cups)
APPROX. COST: 87p or 44p per person

NEED A CHOCOLATE FIX OR JUST WANT A QUICK DESSERT FOR TWO? HERE IS SOMETHING EASY, FUN AND TASTY.

1 Mix everything except the filling together really well and pour into two mugs.

2 In the microwave, heat the first mug for 30 seconds. Add your filling if desired, stir to cover everything with cake mixture, then microwave for another minute. Repeat with the other mug.

INGREDIENTS:

1 egg

4 tbsp self-raising flour

4 tbsp caster sugar

3 tbsp cocoa powder

3 tbsp chocolate spread

3 tbsp milk

3 tbsp vegetable oil

3 tbsp of filling, e.g. marshmallows / chocolate / nuts / raisins (optional)

ENJOY!

CHEF'S TIP:

The cooking times for this recipe are for a 800W microwave. You may need to vary the cooking time depending on your microwave.

LAURA'S STORY

LAURA OLIVER
Brighton & Sussex
Medical School
Medicine

'I WANTED TO REASON THINGS THROUGH ...'

I have wanted to be a doctor for as long as I can remember. When I got into medical school I thought, *'This is it! This is what I've been waiting for all this time!'*

I have always been good with exams but I found this work really tough. In my first year, I failed a couple of modules and was completely gutted. I put so much pressure on myself to do well that I made myself ill. I was homesick and started to wonder what it was all for.

At the beginning of my third year, a guy on my course invited me to a local church. A couple of weeks later, I braved it. I enjoyed meeting new people, listening to talks and questioning things. One evening, a speaker was talking about God's awesome love for us. He was talking of a personal love, of God loving *me* in a way that I couldn't even comprehend.

I knew lots of Christian medics, all of them intelligent people, with stories of how God had worked in their life. I wanted to reason things through, so I signed up for a course where you ate together, watched a DVD and read through the Gospel of Mark. I was able to ask all the hundreds of questions I had.

Before, my life was defined by how well I did in exams, how many friends I had and how others thought of me. Through reading the Gospel I realised that God did love me — and it wasn't a love based on *my performance*. Jesus lived the life I could never live and died the death I deserved to die — now my life is defined by what Jesus *has done for me*. As a result, in the hardest exams I ever had to face, I found myself the least stressed I have ever been!

All in all, university was the best time of my life. I am glad that God helped me then and will help me now as I take my first steps as a junior doctor.

NOW MY LIFE IS DEFINED BY WHAT JESUS HAS DONE FOR ME. AS A RESULT, IN THE HARDEST EXAMS I EVER HAD TO FACE, I FOUND MYSELF THE LEAST STRESSED I HAVE EVER BEEN!

PROFITEROLES

SERVES: 4 (makes about 20 profiteroles)
PREPARATION: 30 minutes
COOKING: 30 minutes
APPROX. COST: £1.46 or 37p per person

INGREDIENTS:
50g butter
150ml water
65g plain flour, sieved
2 eggs, beaten
100g dark chocolate
200ml double cream

Preheat the oven to 190°C. Line a baking tray with some greaseproof paper.

1 Place the butter and water into a saucepan and bring to the boil.

2 Have your flour and a wooden spoon ready to go. As soon as the water is rapidly boiling, add the flour and immediately start mixing. Mix, mix, mix!!! This speedy mixing avoids lumps forming which makes it hard to continue. Eventually the mixture should become a smooth ball that leaves the sides of the pan, then remove from the heat.

3 Add half an egg and mix some more. When it's all fully combined, add another half an egg, and so on. Adding more egg too soon may cause lumps to form. Stop adding egg, though, when you get a dropping consistency.

To check for this, take a big scoop of mixture and allow it to drop off the spoon back into the pan. Now look at the spoon — if there is still a 'ribbon' hanging onto the spoon (see photo), it is ready.

4 Place dessert spoonfuls of mixture on to the baking tray, leaving a little space between each one. Place the tray into the oven and shut the door. Do not open the oven for 20 minutes — the heat causes steam that makes the profiteroles puff up, so we need the heat in the oven.

5 Meanwhile, whip the cream until it forms soft peaks, using a fork or even better a whisk of some sort. Also melt the chocolate. This is best done by putting a small amount of water in a pan and bringing it up to the boil. Turn the heat off as soon as it's reached boiling point, then sit a heatproof bowl containing the chocolate over it.

6 After the profiteroles have been cooking for 20 minutes, check them. They should be golden in colour and light when picked up. If not, give them longer in the oven. Once the profiteroles are ready, cut them open but still joined on one side and put them back in the oven for 5 minutes to crisp up in the middle.

7 Allow the profiteroles to cool. Then fill with cream using a teaspoon and cover with chocolate.

VARIATIONS:

If you don't like cream, use custard or ice cream instead, or just fill the profiteroles with fruit.

For an additional kick of flavour, try adding fruit to the cream—It really freshens up the rich taste.

If you don't like chocolate, try a toffee sauce or fruit sauce.

43

ALED'S STORY

ALED PARRY
University of Exeter,
Cornwall Campus
Renewable Energy

WHERE ARE YOU FROM?

I'm from a small town on the North Welsh coast!

WHAT WERE THE BEST THINGS ABOUT UNI LIFE?

The friends I made. It took a while for us to open up but by my third year I realised how great the guys on my course were. I really enjoyed the independence that uni brought too.

WHAT WERE THE WORST THINGS ABOUT UNI LIFE?

Finishing! It took too long to get to know the people on my course, so when graduation rolled around I wanted to go back and do it all again.

COMING FROM A CHRISTIAN HOME, HOW DID UNIVERSITY CHALLENGE YOUR BELIEFS?

The independence of university gave me the time to think about and question what I believed. Was it my own belief or that of my parents? I read lots. I questioned lots.

WHAT DIFFERENCE HAS THAT QUESTIONING MADE?

I expected to remain apathetic about God while at uni, but after my time of questioning, my faith became deeper. As I read the Bible and discussed stuff with my friend, it became much more than just my upbringing. I have found more peace about what's going to happen in life and I feel more secure about the future because I know it is in God's hands. Life feels richer.

WHAT BIT OF ADVICE WOULD YOU GIVE TO ANYONE HOPING TO GO TO UNI?

Make friends! Even If you are shy and find it hard being away from home. It can be difficult to come out of your shell but it is worth it. By the end of your course you'll hopefully want to do it all again with the mates you've made.

'IT CAN BE DIFFICULT TO COME OUT OF YOUR SHELL BUT IT IS WORTH IT.'

MAKING THE MOST OF STUDENT LIFE

Getting the balance

1. HAVING A GREAT TIME DOESN'T HAVE TO BANKRUPT YOU

Some of the best things in life are free (or nearly free ...). Here's some ideas to start you off:

- Go into **'tourist mode'** — make a day of seeing the sites and freebie museums where you are. Take a camera and record your day out!

- **Escape to the country**. Low on cash? Fed up of being indoors? Grab some mates, get a cheap bus ticket out of town and do some trekking ... or even make it to the seaside!

- See what **'free trials'** you can find online for film downloads/DVDs. Set up a **box-set-a-thon** or series of **film nights** at different halls. Add pizza + popcorn = sorted.

UNI IS HAILED AS ONE OF THOSE UNIQUE STAGES WHERE FREEDOM AND TIME ARE IN YOUR FAVOUR. BUT BALANCING YOUR INTERESTS AND SOCIAL LIFE WITH YOUR DEGREE AND YOUR BANK ACCOUNT IS A TRICKY ONE. HERE'S SOME FOOD FOR THOUGHT TO HELP YOU MAKE THE MOST OF YOUR STUDENT-DAYS!

- Have a **board game fest**. Whether it's an all-night battle of monopoly or a retro family favourite (Buckaroo, anyone?), buy it once (or pinch it from home) and that's an addictive night in for all.

- **Go abroad!** Most students get the jet-setting bug and crave ways to explore the world for pennies. What about teaching English or volunteering your skills at a camp or school over the summer? Expenses are often covered and some offer 'pocket money' on top. It's a great way to meet new people, see a different culture and get some international experience for your CV! Check out: www.leo-lingo.de, www.englishexp.co.uk & www.campamerica.co.uk

2. DON'T BE PUSHED INTO THINGS YOU DON'T REALLY WANT TO DO …

Your friends will get over it if you say no.

3. GET STUCK IN

If you have a desire to join the rugby team or knitting squad but your mates are rowing enthusiasts, sign up for what suits you. You'll make a new set of mates to your course or flatmates and it will add variety to your week!

4. A DEGREE YOU SAY?

The aim of being at university is to gain the best degree you can — it's worth remembering. The NUS website has some helpful articles and tips for revising, speed reading, dissertations and more.

5. TIME OUT

Are you a social animal who only stops for loo breaks, or do you restore your energy in a quiet, darkened room? Whichever you are, taking some time to rest and 'stop' will aid your social life and your degree.

6. SUPPORT

Some people take to change like a duck to water, but they are the exception and not the rule. It can take a while to adjust to life at university and settle into a course. It is important to get help if you are feeling stressed. A tutor, the Student Union, a chaplain or the student help services where you are will be able to point you to the right support for you.

> THE AIM OF BEING AT UNIVERSITY IS TO GAIN THE BEST DEGREE YOU CAN — IT'S WORTH REMEMBERING.

FROZEN COOKIES

THIS COOKIE DOUGH IS BRILLIANT BECAUSE IT FREEZES REALLY WELL. IF FRIENDS COME OVER OR YOU JUST WANT SOME WARM COOKIES, YOU CAN SLICE SOME OFF AND COOK IT STRAIGHT FROM FROZEN.

MAKES: about 15 cookies
PREPARATION: 15 minutes
COOKING: 15 minutes
APPROX. COST: 80p or 5p per cookie plus 15–70p depending on your filling choice

INGREDIENTS:

120g butter, softened

90g caster sugar

1 egg yolk

120g plain flour

½ tsp bicarbonate of soda

¼ tsp salt

210g of filling, e.g. chocolate (chopped in pieces) / oats, chocolate and nuts/ mixed nuts and raisins ...

Preheat the oven to 175°C and line a baking tray with greaseproof paper (if cooking now).

1 Cream the butter and sugar together until light and fluffy by beating it with a wooden spoon or using an electric mixer.

2 Add the yolk and mix well.

3 Add the flour, bicarbonate of soda and salt along with your filling and mix until everything is combined.

4 If you want to freeze all or some of it for later, roll that dough into a cylinder and cover with cling film. This will freeze for up to 3 months.

5 Otherwise, put tablespoon amounts of the dough on the baking tray, leaving a little space for each one to spread. Cook for 10 minutes, then turn the tray 180° and cook for a final 2 minutes or until the cookies are golden brown on top. Allow to cool.

To cook from frozen, take the dough out of the freezer and slice it into 'little finger' thick cookies, just less than 1cm thick. Then follow the cooking instructions.

KAYODE'S STORY

KAYODE ADENIRAN
University of Sussex
Law

I stayed on at my school sixth form to study my A levels and as a result was fairly at home in my surroundings. I was excited to go to uni and experience something new. I was looking for that independence!

When I first made it to uni, the biggest challenges for me were probably more practical than emotional. Things like washing my clothes and registering with the doctors were all preceded with a call to the parents asking how to go about these things! The bonuses far outweighed the negatives though — and not being accountable to anyone was pretty fun. For me, being able to order as much fast food as I wanted was paradise.

I grew up in a church-going family and my mum and dad were heavily involved in prison ministry. As a child and in my teens, it's not that I had any internal disagreements with the Christian faith but I just kind of assented to things 'you're supposed to believe in'. Yet the way I lived my life didn't match my alleged beliefs. When I got to uni, there was a period of uncertainty that I think most students can empathise with — I had bigger questions to life, like, *'What am I doing at university?'* and *'What's it all for?'* Was I in a factory line of people trying to have a good time, get good grades, get a good job and then have a family? *'Was there anything more?'* You could see an emptiness in people around me; there was a darkness there — including in myself.

I suppose it was then that I started looking for answers. I wanted to see if all I had heard about God was really true, so I read about Jesus and hungered to experience a living relationship with him. As a result my desires started to change and I was looking at the world with new lenses, I guess. I wasn't defined by what I did or how I acted anymore — but I was defined by Jesus Christ and his love, life and death.

'I WANTED TO SEE IF ALL I HAD HEARD ABOUT GOD WAS REALLY TRUE ...'

FIND OUT MORE

You were probably given this little book by someone from your college Christian Union! I hope you find it helpful as you venture into university life. It has lots of recipes and tips that I could have done with. If you have been interested in some of the student stories, I would urge you to find out more. Look into whether Jesus really existed, whether he is who he claimed to be and whether he actually loves you as an individual and died (and rose from the dead!) for you. Reading the book of Luke or John in the New Testament is a great place to start, or why not read a book like *Mere Christianity* by the Narnia guy (C.S. Lewis). He sums up the Christian faith pretty well — and even if you don't agree with it, it's worth a read.

When you do get to university, go along to a Christian Union event! Anyone is welcome and it's a great place to debate, explore and find answers to the big questions of life, as well as to make friends …

EVERYONE WANTS THE BEST UNIVERSITY EXPERIENCE. JESUS SAID, 'I HAVE COME THAT THEY MAY HAVE LIFE, AND HAVE IT TO THE FULL!'[4]

Kayode Adeniran, Law student at the University of Sussex

[4] John 10:10.

If the student stories in **Beyond Beans On Toast** have sparked some questions, here are some helpful places to explore a bit more:

- Get connected with the Christian Union at your university: **uccf.org.uk/find-your-cu**

- Examine the evidence of the life and purpose of Jesus Christ: **uncover.org.uk**

- Watch a short video explaining the heart of Christianity in 5 minutes, called '3-2-1 — The story of God, the world and you': **three-two-one.org**

- Read the Bible online — a Gospel like Luke or John is a good place to start: **biblegateway.com**

- Contact 10ofthose.com to be sent something to read and think through: **info@10ofthose.com**

Alternatively, get in touch with us at Festive: **info@festive.org.uk** We would love to hear how you found this book and would be happy to help you find out more.

a division of **10** **of those**.com

10Publishing is the publishing house of **10ofThose**.
It is committed to producing quality Christian resources that are biblical and accessible.

www.10ofthose.com is our online retail arm selling thousands of quality books at discounted prices.

For information contact: **sales@10ofthose.com**
or check out our website: **www.10ofthose.com**